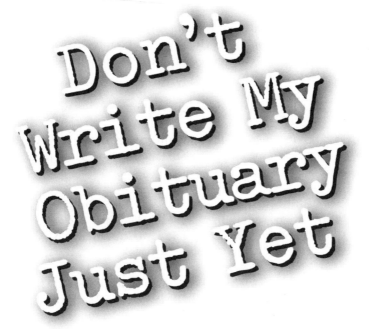

Don't Write My Obituary Just Yet

Inspiring Faith Stories for Older Adults

Missy Buchanan

UPPER
ROOM BOOKS®
NASHVILLE

Cover and interior design: Nancy Terzian / Buckinghorse Design
Cover image: Big Cheese Photo
First printing: 2011

LIBRARY OF CONGRESS CATALOGING-IN-PUBLICATION
Buchanan, Missy.
  Don't write my obituary just yet : inspiring faith stories for older adults / Missy Buchanan.
    p. cm.
  ISBN 978-0-8358-1046-3
  1. Older people—Religious life. 2. Aging—Religious aspects—Christianity. I. Title.
  BV4580.B78 2011
  242'.65—dc22   2010045441

Printed in the United States of America

I gratefully dedicate this book

to the men and women

who graciously opened their homes and hearts

to share their life stories with me

that I might share them with others.

Your tears and laughter,

your faith and perseverance

inspire us all.

Contents

Introduction

I love stories. I love to hear them. I love to share them. Stories help us understand things we would otherwise not understand. They help us remember things we would otherwise forget. Good stories leave an imprint on our hearts and inspire us to live differently.

The stories in this book have been collected from real-life older adults who are still living with purpose in their late years. They are ordinary, faith-filled people from all walks of life. Some are active; others face physical or mental limitations. All are dealing with the common aches and pains and losses associated with longevity.

Some stories are about people I have known all my life. Others tell about folks I met as I traveled the country to speak to older-adult groups. A few describe seniors who were referred to me by ministers. All are inspiring!

< 7 >

Betty P.
Finishing strong

* * *

When I sit down to talk with Betty, she is in the midst of a difficult life transition. During the last year, her husband passed away following a brief illness. For sixty-one years they had loved each other with a longer-than-forever kind of love. Now she has moved into a one-bedroom apartment in a retirement community, leaving behind the home they had built as newlyweds.

At age eighty-six, Betty admits it was hard to walk away from the place where they had reared their three children and created memories, but she and her husband had discussed the matter before he died. Because of health issues and safety concerns, the two had decided a move would be in her best interest.

As Betty proudly gives me a tour of her lovely living quarters, it quickly becomes obvious that she has made up her mind to dwell on all that

< 8 >

is positive about her new life. There's no yard work or home repair to worry about. She cooks only when she wants. She makes new friends and participates in a wide variety of activities, including swimming and brain exercise. By the time Betty has finished her litany of pluses, I am ready to move in myself. Mostly, though, I am in awe of her marvelous attitude.

I have to remind myself that life has not always turned out as Betty might have liked. She has had heart bypass surgery. Each day she deals with the effects of diabetes, high blood pressure, retinopathy, and hearing loss. Certainly she would have liked more time to spend with her husband, more healthy days to explore new places, more energy to keep up with her grandchildren and great-grandchildren. But the way Betty sees it, she has two choices: either whine and complain or embrace this stage of life and finish strong. As a matter of faith, she chooses the latter.

Sitting down to talk with Betty in the living room, I notice a curio cabinet filled with a large collection of bells. Some are crystal; others are porcelain or metal. Almost all are mementos

< 9 >

from places where she and her husband traveled, including Europe and Australia, China and Hawaii. When I call attention to an especially beautiful glass bell with threads of gold, she tells me that it came from Venice, Italy. Actually it was made from hand-blown glass on the nearby island of Murano, Italy. Studying the bells more closely, I find my heart uplifted. Betty and her husband had always lived comfortably but modestly. Travel was a small extravagant pleasure they shared with great joy and passion, and it made my heart happy just thinking of their life experiences.

Truly Betty models for others an attitude of gracious acceptance of her situation. She sees aging as part of God's plan for humankind. Rather than something to dread, aging presents an opportunity for God to reveal God's strength. Betty is running the race of life and finishing strong. I am confident that she will one day hear the words, "Well done, good and faithful servant." And when she does, all the bells of heaven will ring.

< 10 >

Philippians 3:12-14

I don't mean to say that I have already achieved these things or that I have already reached perfection. But I press on to possess that perfection for which Christ Jesus first possessed me. No, dear brothers and sisters, I have not achieved it, but I focus on this one thing: Forgetting the past and looking forward to what lies ahead, I press on to reach the end of the race and receive the heavenly prize for which God, through Christ Jesus, is calling us.

Prayer

O bountiful God,
You know that change is hard. Still you know my every need. With each new day, help me to press on toward the goal that lies ahead. Fill me with anticipation and help me to finish strong. Amen.

< 11 >

Winston

The river runs through

* * *

Winston is a winsome eighty-four-year-old man with dashing good looks and a fondness for teasing. He's also articulate and disciplined, making it easy to understand why he succeeded as a businessman until he finally retired at seventy. Even so, Winston considers he was just blessed to be in the right place at the right time.

Born in the midst of the Great Depression, Winston was the only child of a frail mother and an alcoholic father who abandoned the family when Winston was seven years old. His mother later passed away at the early age of thirty-nine. Tempered by a difficult childhood, Winston applied the hard-learned lessons of personal responsibility to become valedictorian of his high school and a star athlete in college before joining the military.

< 12 >

As we sit down to talk at his riverside home, only a few months have passed since Winston's wife of more than sixty years passed away following a long battle with cancer. His voice begins to tremble as he describes adjusting to life without her. She had been his companion and a great influence in his faith journey. Moments later, though, his eyes dance with a hint of mischief, and the room fills again with his hearty laugh and yet another tale of their life together.

According to Winston, his life was forged by faith from an early age. He remembers going to church with his grandparents when he was a child. Later, as a married man, he embraced church life wherever he and his wife lived. I glance at a shelf lined with study Bibles and commentaries. Winston notices and tells me about teaching a college-aged Sunday school class when he and his wife were newlyweds. Even at this stage of life, Winston easily recites long passages of scripture from memory. He is a certified lay speaker, a Sunday school teacher, and a participant in a men's organization in his local congregation. With a razor-sharp wit, it's no wonder that church youth are drawn to him too.

< 13 >

Though his general health is good, Winston cannot drive due to deteriorating eyesight. Learning to depend on others to take him places doesn't come easily to this can-do guy, but he has accepted the situation with grace and a big dose of humor. By his own admission, he is not a golfer, a hunter, or a fisherman, but he finds great joy in being a generous philanthropist. And this mind-set has been carried down to his children. They've started a new tradition: instead of exchanging typical Christmas gifts, family members now buy one another stocking stuffers and make donations to favorite charities and church ministries. From the stories he tells, Winston's relationships with family and friends clearly remain vital to his well-being.

Before I leave Winston's home, he tells me one last story about a group of men who will be meeting at his home the next morning. Like clockwork, six older adult men gather around his dining table each Monday morning for coffee, fellowship, and prayer. I could easily imagine a rowdy bunch of older men nudging one another and laughing like those who have a long history of shared experiences. The funny thing is,

< 14 >

Winston has known them only for the eight years that he's lived in the community. Like their friend, the men have discovered that friendships in late life can be meaningful and rewarding, especially if they are built on a strong spiritual foundation.

Giving a farewell hug to my new friend, I think to myself that we all need a Winston in our life—someone willing to stay fresh, who laughs a lot, who rolls up his pants legs and wades into the river of life.

Revelation 22:1

Then the angel showed me a river with the water of life, clear as crystal, flowing from the throne of God and of the Lamb.

Prayer

God of everlasting life,
Even as I celebrate the sweet remembrance of loved ones who have gone on to glory, give me courage to keep living. On days when my life is bone-dry, walk with me to the river of life that I might live fully in the present. Amen.

< 15 >

Jewell

Blind with
20/20 vision

* * *

Jewell can put a smile on anybody's face. In fact, there's something about this ninety-year-old woman that reminds me of Mrs. Santa Claus, at least the way I picture her in my mind's eye. She's round and jolly with rosy cheeks and sparkling eyes. And just like I imagine Mrs. Claus, Jewell is friendly and warm, welcoming strangers as if they are long-lost family.

But life hasn't always been so cheery. As a child, Jewell lived a hardscrabble life, growing up with ten brothers and sisters in a very poor family. Later she married and had three children of her own. By the time she had grown old, she had mourned the loss of two husbands, a grown son, a grandson, and a great-grandson.

Along the journey, Jewell also experienced a debilitating stroke that left doctors scratching

< 16 >

their heads, amazed that she had even survived. After months of speech and physical therapy, she finally regained her speech and the ability to walk with assistance. But the stroke left her legally blind, so that now she sees only shadowy shapes.

In spite of limited vision, Jewell still picks up her yarn and needles and knits by feel instead of sight. She sits for hours in her favorite recliner, creating colorful scarves, shawls, and hats for friends and family.

When I ask others what they love most about Jewell, their answers echo the same theme. It's the way she fastens her mind on all that is good in life. If tablemates complain that the chicken is overdone, Jewell expresses thanks she didn't have to prepare it. If the room temperature is a little too chilly for some, she wraps a shawl around her shoulders and refuses to complain. She laughs easily and often at her own forgetfulness. It's no wonder that both family and staff members at her assisted living center adore being in her presence.

As I sit across from Jewell in her cozy room, I ask about her positive outlook. Not surprisingly she shrugs it off, saying she's lived a charmed life. But it's more than that. Jewell's cheerfulness

< 17 >

is birthed in a grateful and generous spirit. She knows that God alone is the source of her blessings. Jewell may be legally blind, but clearly her vision is 20/20.

A cheerful heart is good medicine,
but a broken spirit saps a person's strength.

Prayer

O God,
Help me this day to have a cheerful heart. To see the best in people as you do, to remember that you are the source of every blessing in my long life. Though my face is wrinkled and my eyes are dim, let me find ways to give myself to others. Amen.

< 18 >

Jim and Betty

Just do it!

* * *

It doesn't take long to discover Jim and Betty's simple, one-word credo for living a long, meaningful life: volunteer. The way these two see life, there is always a need somewhere. Find it and fill it. Jim and Betty continue to live out that philosophy, even in their late years. Like a pair of heat-seeking missiles, they target yet another opportunity to serve others.

Married for fifty-four years, Jim and Betty describe their life together as a series of coincidences or, rather, "God incidences." They met in a Sunday school class, and their friendship blossomed into a deep love still evident as they laugh and finish each other's sentences. But they grow serious when they talk about the importance of being part of a church family. With glistening eyes, they recount the story of their infant daughter's death years ago.

< 19 >

Their church community wrapped its arms around them, carrying them through to brighter days. Jim and Betty have never forgotten the lesson about selflessly serving others.

Now mission projects excite them most. From building water purification systems in Mexican border towns to recruiting greeters for Sunday morning services, no job is too big or too small for Jim and Betty's involvement. They talk passionately about multigenerational missions where they work alongside teenagers and younger adults. In fact, since their son and his family have moved nearby, they hope to model volunteerism in a way that will influence their two grandsons.

For years Betty and Jim drove their RV to mission projects, especially to sites without electricity or running water. Sometimes Jim would work on construction projects while Betty prepared meals for the crew. They've participated in cleanup and rebuilding efforts following hurricanes and construction projects in impoverished areas. They are not about to stop now! Jim and Betty giggle at the idea that most people think they are younger than their respective ages, eighty-four and eighty-five. Betty

< 20 >

is surprised she's lived so long considering other family members have died at much younger ages. She credits volunteerism as a primary reason she is still living a full and productive life.

Although they can't do all they once did, Jim and Betty firmly believe that getting your mind off yourself and onto someone else will improve your attitude. Growing old is no reason to withdraw from the world. When asked what energizes them for a new day, Jim laughs and responds that it's the clock. He means it's time to get up and find someone who has a need.

Isaiah 6:8

Then I heard the Lord asking, "Whom should I send as a messenger to this people? Who will go for us?" I said, "Here I am. Send me."

Prayer

God of the ages,
Some days I feel I have outlived my purpose. I wonder how I can contribute anything to the world. Open my old eyes to new opportunities to serve. In serving others I find purpose. Amen.

< 21 >

John

Passionate persistence

* * *

Not quite eighty, John could have been a poster boy for active older adults. Everyone in his independent living facility admired him. He was strong, intelligent, and full of energy. A retired engineer, he had traveled the world and had a great passion for learning. Then came a stroke.

The news sent everyone at the senior residence center into a tizzy. How could this have happened to John? He had done all the right things. He ate healthy food, exercised daily, and followed the doctor's directions to a tee. He went to Sunday school every week and sometimes even taught the class. Yet, this once-vibrant man now was going through extensive rehabilitation in hopes of regaining his strength and his ability to walk.

Actually it was not the first time John had been faced with an overwhelming challenge.

< 22 >

Just a few years earlier, he had dealt with the devastating loss of his wife. They had been each other's best friend, and when she died, life felt strangely off balance. Even so, he made up his mind to honor her memory by living well.

The idea of doing rehabilitative therapy for long months ahead left John feeling discouraged. It was depressing to see the row of other older adults in wheelchairs, waiting their turn to do exercises that, everyone hoped, would help them regain their abilities too.

No doubt John was tempted to wither up and die, but he tackled his therapy with a faith-filled determination. Over time, he emerged from the darkness. Looking back, he recalls the unexpected blessings he found in rehab. He made new friends with patients and therapists. He discovered an artistic gift for painting that he didn't know he had. Most important, he found that passionate persistence pays off.

Today John uses a cane when he walks. He tires more easily than before, but he has recaptured much of his prior ability. Best of all, the stroke did not steal his insatiable desire for learning. In fact, it has led him to new pursuits.

< 23 >

Each week when I visit with John, I look forward to hearing his latest tale about old movies, surfing the Web for historical information, and painting beautiful scenes of places he and his wife had once visited. John knows that God can bring new life to the lifeless.

Isaiah 40:31

Those who trust in the LORD will find new strength.
   They will soar high on wings like eagles.
They will run and not grow weary.
   They will walk and not faint.

Prayer

O God,
When depression seeps into the marrow of my bones, rekindle my passion for living. Encourage me to make the most of what life has dealt me. Though my body falters, I am still me. Give me strength to do things I don't think I can. Let me be light that pushes back the darkness. Amen.

< 24 >

Ginny

From Job to joy

* * *

Ginny sometimes feels like Job. In the span of her eighty-one years, a series of unbelievable trials and losses has tested her faith repeatedly. It seems that just as she has cleared one hurdle, another one pops up. When I look into the eyes of my friend, I can't help wondering how much adversity one person can take, especially in the late years of life.

Ginny is a former second-grade teacher who has nurtured thousands of children throughout her long teaching career. As she was edging closer to retirement, Ginny's husband died suddenly of a heart attack. For a while, joy drained away from her life. Trusting God did not always come easy, she says, but she clung to her faith and slogged through days of deep darkness. In time, the gloom started to lift and life brightened. She began to dream new dreams and even married for a second time.

< 25 >

Then came the diagnosis every woman dreads: breast cancer. After surgery and a grueling regimen of chemotherapy, Ginny felt as if she finally had reached the calm after a storm. That's when she suffered a debilitating stroke. She completed months of strenuous rehabilitation. Then her second husband died of a heart attack, leaving her widowed once again.

Life seemed to be playing a very mean trick. Ginny's cancer returned. There was another mastectomy, followed by melanoma, heart problems, and diabetes. Today, barely a week goes by without a visit to the doctor or another round of medical tests.

Ginny has had more than her share of heartache and uncertainty, and on some days she is tempted to cry out, "Why me?" As we sit and talk about her life, I see a sheen of tears on her face. Yet she is grinning, even laughing. She resists self-pity because she knows it can eat you up like an out-of-control virus. She knows too that God's hope is stronger than her desperation.

Ginny keeps on praising God's faithfulness. She is grateful for knowledgeable doctors and medical procedures that have saved her life. She delights in

< 26 >

her granddaughter's latest accomplishments. Every day she hugs other seniors and encourages them to count their blessings in spite of their afflictions.

It is no surprise that people are drawn to Ginny's tenacity and her kind ways. In a life filled with uncertainty, she is confident in her future. She knows that ultimately God will set things right.

James 5:11

We give great honor to those who endure under suffering. For instance, you know about Job, a man of great endurance. You can see how the Lord was kind to him at the end, for the Lord is full of tenderness and mercy.

Prayer

Father God,
Sometimes I feel as though I have reached a breaking point. I want to shout, "Why me?" Life can be so unfair. Give me unexpected strength to get through times of uncertainty. Then use my life that others may find encouragement in my perseverance. I am confident that the best is yet to be. Amen.

< 27 >

Betty J.

Stepping out in faith

* * *

An energetic octogenarian, Betty is the much-loved matriarch of her extended family. Everyone knows she loves sparkly high-heeled shoes, a good indication that this redhead doesn't take herself too seriously. She is a former history teacher with a magical laugh and a streak of endearing independence.

For all of their married life, Betty and her husband shared a love of travel, even when others chuckled at their unorthodox ways. Often he would pilot their small plane to remote destinations in Central America just to experience the nontouristy side of life. Over the years Betty learned to fully embrace her husband's adventuresome travel ideas. Nowadays she even giggles about the time they slept in sleeping bags under their airplane in a secluded Mexican village.

Betty's sense of adventure has served her well

< 28 >

through the years, even in tough times. She has survived tremendous heartbreak, especially in the sunset years of her life. When her husband was diagnosed with cancer, she became his daily caregiver. Then after forty-two years of marriage, he passed away. A few years later, she faced the heartrending sorrow of burying her only grandson, a teenager tragically killed in an automobile wreck. Not long afterward, her middle-aged son lost his battle with cancer.

After the deaths of three beloved family members, Betty could have been tempted to retreat into herself and remain glum. But that is not her way. Instead she turned to her faith and became a leaning post for others.

Recently Betty fell in her home and fractured her pelvis. Her doctor said she would need rehabilitation therapy for several weeks as an in-house patient. At first, Betty resisted the idea of going to a rehab facility, clinging to the notion that she could heal just fine at home. She later admitted she had been unsettled by an image she'd conjured up in her mind of hallways lined with feeble old people.

Once she was into the full swing of the rehab

< 29 >

though, it didn't take long for Betty to have an epiphany. As she progressed through the exercises and shared time with other residents, she noticed a woman sitting alone in her wheelchair with her shoulders slumped and her eyes fixed on the floor. Ordinarily Betty would have hesitated to initiate a conversation with the woman, fearing she would not know what to say or do. However, on this day, her adventurous spirit led her to take a risk.

Betty rolled her wheelchair over and commented on the beautifully stitched red cardinals on the woman's sweater. The frail woman's eyes brightened as she lifted her head to look at Betty. She began to tell the story about being known in her neighborhood as the redbird lady because she had cared for the birds. In that brief encounter, Betty says, she felt a nudge from God, reminding her that she still has purpose as an encourager to others. From that moment on, she began to seek those who needed an encouraging word.

These days Betty lives independently at home, fully armed with fall-prevention measures. She's even traded in her sparkly high-heeled shoes for

< 30 >

a pair of safety-conscious metallic gold sneakers. But make no mistake. Betty is stepping out of her comfort zone because she knows God will show her another opportunity to uplift someone else.

Ephesians 4:29

Don't use foul or abusive language. Let everything you say be good and helpful, so that your words will be an encouragement to those who hear them.

Prayer

Friend of the aged,
On this day, nudge me out of my comfort zone. Focus my mind on others. Give me words to build them up. Unleash your spirit and lead me on this great adventure of life. Amen.

< 31 >

Elizabeth

'Tis a gift
to be simple

* * *

I first met Elizabeth in a quaint community nestled in the rural countryside, not far from the farm where she and her husband reared their seven children. Within moments of our introduction, I could sense that she is just as others had described—a person of great faith who finds contentment in the simple things of life.

Elizabeth points to a stand of trees outside her window as we take our seats. In soft tones she tells me that they are dressed in her favorite shades of autumn. Soon she is sharing a story about her faith journey, specifically how she first discovered God in nature.

As a young child, one of Elizabeth's many chores was to assist in planting the vegetables on her family's farm. She would make holes in the dirt with her little finger, then drop in tiny radish

< 32 >

seeds and push the rich soil to cover them. I could see her aging eyes begin to dance as she described the excitement of waiting for the small heart-shaped leaves to push their way through the fertile soil. While kneeling in the dirt, Elizabeth had also learned to kneel her heart before the Creator.

I soon discover that spending time with Elizabeth is like putting on a pair of special high-definition glasses. Suddenly you see all of nature in the full glory of sharpened images and amplified colors. For Elizabeth, God's presence is never more clear than in the place where sun and soil come together to feed the soul.

Just a few hours after our visit, I discovered a note under my door at the guest quarters where I was staying in her retirement community. Elizabeth had written to thank me for our time together. She had included a few poems that she had written with beautiful words about silos in soft, filtered light and corn standing in straight rows in the fields.

By the time I finished reading her letter, my eyes were misty. I could sense her radiant aliveness. I knew that Elizabeth's mark of wisdom is a deep understanding that all living things

< 33 >

were created to glorify the Creator. In many ways Elizabeth's life is a bit of a paradox. From the simple things in nature she has harvested a life of abundant contentment and joy.

On the day following our talk, Elizabeth stood on the steps inside her church, surrounded by a gaggle of her great-grandchildren. In honor of her one-hundredth birthday, they sang with her the simple words: "Jesus loves me! This I know." It seems a perfect song for one with childlike faith who surrenders to the wonder of it all.

Psalm 19:1

The heavens proclaim the glory of God.
The skies display his craftsmanship.

Prayer

O God,
Turn my eyes upon the details of your handiwork. You have created a world that proves miraculously new if only I will look. As my body fades like a winter sunset, awaken my senses. Let me get lost in the wonder of your creation. Amen.

< 34 >

Ed

The rest of
the story

* * *

A young mother came to the church office asking for Ed, a ninety-year-old man who had helped her during a financially difficult time. She remembered the kindness of the older man who served with the church's ministry to people in crisis. Now, a year later, the woman had both a good job and a bright future. She had come to thank Ed for his support and to pay back money the church had provided to assist with expenses for utilities and rent.

Ed's eyes rimmed with tears and his voice quivered with emotion as he heard the young woman's success story. He was overwhelmed by her act of responsibility and courage. Truth be known, this retired United States Air Force colonel has a heart of pure gold.

Ed had a long, distinguished military career that included a stint as a director of flight

< 35 >

training. Each Veterans Day weekend when my church salutes those who have served in the armed forces, I am reminded of his sacrifice and service. When the Air Force song begins to play, my eyes track Ed as he proudly moves to the front of the sanctuary. Even though his frame has begun to stoop a bit, he is a commanding figure.

Ed is both an astonishingly deep thinker and a persistent student of scripture. Every month he takes a turn teaching a senior adult Sunday school class. By studying scripture and reading in-depth commentaries, he guards against mental and spiritual sluggishness. He also participates in multigenerational Bible studies, just as he did for so many years alongside his wife.

Ed's wife of many decades passed away a few years ago. In mourning her loss, he felt God's hand clearly guiding him toward new opportunities. Once an avid fisherman, Ed now spends much of his time volunteering at a community food pantry and resale shop where he regularly sorts, catalogs, and stacks nonperishable food items and household goods. At the same time, he remains involved in his church's own outreach ministry to help those in urgent need.

< 36 >

When I ask Ed what his work at the food pantry means to him, a look of satisfaction spreads across his face. He says it's not about doing mindless tasks. It's about finding purpose in late life by staying connected to the needs of the community.

Certainly Ed has many endearing qualities. He is intelligent, loyal, and witty. But what makes the biggest impact on others is his colossal heart. Just ask the young woman who returned to the church in search of the older man who had so lovingly assisted her when she needed it most.

Ephesians 6:7

Work with enthusiasm, as though you were working for the Lord rather than for people.

Prayer

Compassionate God,
Give me a holy curiosity about your Word. Even as I age there is much to learn. Show me how to live out the lessons of scripture. Point me toward a new opportunity to help others. Then give me the courage to do it. Amen.

< 37 >

Inez

Dreaming a new dream

* * *

When I think back on my early childhood, random impressions and memories stick on the walls of my mind. One special image is of Inez, a fixture in the church I grew up in many years ago. Miss Inez, as I referred to her then, taught in the children's Sunday school department for decades, often alongside my mother. Today there is still a sweetness about Inez that somehow makes you feel better about the world.

Now ninety-seven years old, Inez has been widowed for many years. Though she lives alone in her own home, a large family surrounds her with love, a family that includes twenty-one great-grandchildren and two great-great grandchildren. In spite of her extended years, Inez's mind is sharp as a tack. She is also active in a senior adult choir and a community art council.

< 38 >

A number of years ago Inez discovered a gift she'd never known she had. While on a trip with her husband, she bought a paint-by-number kit to pass the time while her husband fished. Little did she know that simple kit would stir a creative passion in her and unleash an artistic gift. Eventually she would sell her original artwork to a client base spread across the country.

For Inez art is more than something to keep her busy. Art is about dreaming new dreams and creating something new. Over the years she has honed her natural gift, stretching far beyond the beginner's how-to art kit. She reports that her imagination is often fired up by nostalgic images from the early days of her town's settlement. She loves painting street scenes from history that she actually lived, including old frame buildings and dirt roads. But she is also drawn to images of wildflowers in the late afternoon light or wisteria that winds itself into a purple canopy. No matter the subject of her artwork, each piece represents a relationship between her passionate heart and the need to express.

Though some people struggle against growing old, Inez has slipped quietly into old age with

< 39 >

beautiful grace and acceptance. This woman of deep, unyielding faith believes it's never too late to dream. At this late stage of life, she is glad to be liberated from the clock, because time spent painting goes unmarked.

I can't help noticing a palpable sense of joy when Inez talks about her love of painting—of starting with a blank canvas and an array of paint hues, then creating a one-of-a-kind expression. To me it is much like Inez's life—a unique masterpiece of the Creator.

Ephesians 2:10

For we are God's masterpiece. He has created us anew in Christ Jesus, so we can do the good things he planned for us long ago.

Prayer

Creator God,
Don't let me waste time at this stage of life.
Renew my spirit and let me feel your presence.
You have created me in your image. I too am made to create. Prompt my heart to dream new dreams this day. Amen.

< 40 >

Jim and Nancy

In sickness
and in health

* * *

From the first time you meet Jim and Nancy, you know they have been sweethearts for a very long time. A former athlete, he is a gentleman who still opens the door for her. She is a beauty whose eyes twinkle at the sight of him. They met in college and have been married for fifty-five years. The truth is, their love story is better than any made-for-TV movie.

Jim, a retired educator and school principal, earned a reputation as a fair-minded but tough administrator, gaining the respect of teachers, parents, and students alike. Some might call him a straight-arrow kind of guy. They would be right. He unashamedly honors God, family, country, and the can-do spirit. Simply put, Jim believes in working hard, playing fair, and loving much.

< 41 >

For all these years, Nancy has been Jim's wife, his sidekick, and his favorite fishing partner. With a sunny disposition, she exudes kindness and joy even on the dreariest of days. During the past few years, Nancy's mind has begun to wander into the murky fog of an Alzheimer's-like dementia.

When Jim and Nancy received the initial diagnosis, they took the news in stride, vowing to keep living as they always had for as long as they could. Besides fishing, they enjoyed gardening and attending sporting events, especially those involving their three grandsons. They had also been very active in many ministries of their church.

Over the last year Nancy's condition has deteriorated. Her dependence on Jim and others increases as her memory slips. Still, with the help of family and friends, Jim and Nancy adapt to the ever-changing landscape of dementia.

For as long as I can remember, Nancy has sung alto in the church choir. More than a decade ago, when I was still in the choir, I often sat beside Nancy during rehearsals. We'd giggle together when the basses came in a measure too early. Today Jim faithfully brings

< 42 >

her to choir rehearsals where she sits between two choir members who act as her guardian angels, assisting her when needed. Each Sunday morning, she dons a choir robe and sings with a joyful heart as best she can. Her fellow choir members say that even as Nancy's mental ability has diminished, she unfailingly walks into the choir room with a big smile and announces, "God is good." Perhaps the minister of music captures it best when he says that Nancy's spirit does not need a lot of words to shine through.

Jim has taken over almost all the household duties, and at times others worry that he is stretching himself too thin for a man of seventy-seven years. But they also respect his devotion to his wife and best friend. Certainly these sunset years are not easy for the pair. No matter what the future holds, their faith is strong. Jim knows that one day the vibrant woman Nancy used to be will be fully released in the presence of God. Until then and forever more, she remains the light of his life.

Proverbs 12:4

A worthy wife is a crown for her husband.

< 43 >

Merciful God,

I am thankful for a long life filled with the love of a companion. When unexpected trials seem to swallow my joy, keep my eyes on you, knowing there will be a better tomorrow. Let me love with your love. Make me strong with your strength. Give me eyes to see beyond this day to eternity. Amen.

< 44 >

Flo

No terrible
twist of fate

* * *

Those who know Flo best likely would describe her as an Annie Oakley on Medicare. She's a straight-shootin' kind of woman who doesn't like raisins or uppity people. But under that matter-of-fact exterior beats a heart of pure gold.

Flo never had children and has been widowed for years, but she is blessed with a loving extended family. Every week when I visit her at her senior residence, I am reminded of her unique gift—a powerful memory that many would call a steel-trap mind. In fact, talking with Flo is much like perusing the pages of an encyclopedia. From presidential trivia to little-known historical events, my own fact checking proves her to be right again and again.

Not long ago I took Flo to visit her tablemate who had moved temporarily to a rehabilitation center while she recovered from a fall. I still

< 45 >

remember Flo's expression as she took her first ride in a glass elevator. Her childlike awe was contagious even for the employees who shared the ride. By the time Flo rolled her walker out of the elevator, all of us were giddy. Her unrestrained joy had transformed ordinary routine into a glimpse of heaven.

I am grateful that my life has intertwined with Flo's during the last decade. I think about her perspective on growing old and realize that she doesn't look at aging as some terrible twist of fate. She does not wring her hands over bleak prospects of what might happen tomorrow. Though she knows firsthand the challenges that come with physical decline, she simply accepts growing old as part of God's divine plan. And since God created aging, she knows there is a purpose.

John 15:10-11

"When you obey my commandments, you remain in my love, just as I obey my Father's commandments and remain in his love. I have told you these things so that you will be filled with my joy. Yes, your joy will overflow!"

< 46 >

Prayer

God of the aged,
You designed the aging process. You fashioned
our bodies to change over time. Help me to see
aging through the eyes of faith. You still want
to use my hands to give to others. You want to
comfort others through my voice. You want your
love to shine through my face so that others will
see your glory. Flood me with your holy light and
let it be so. Amen.

< 47 >

Marlin

When all you have
is more than enough

* * *

Marlin spends much of his time sitting in a wheelchair, looking out the window of his room in a skilled nursing facility. After ninety-nine years, his body is thin and frail. At times his posture is one people fear most: sagging head, chin to chest, lost in time.

Until a few years ago Marlin lived independently in a senior apartment where he had moved after his wife passed away. Each morning he went to a nearby community center where he played dominoes and cards for hours at a time. He laughed with other old men and shared tales of days gone by. Then came a sudden health crisis.

Not long after he was hospitalized, Marlin moved to the nursing home where he now shares a tidy but institutional room with another resident. He is dependent on caregivers to help

< 48 >

him bathe and dress. Getting from the wheelchair to his bed drains what little energy he has left at the end of the day. Even though his body is weak, his faith remains amazingly strong.

Still he asks himself the inevitable, hard questions. *What's the point of living for so long when it seems there's so little I can contribute? Why do some people grow old with relative ease while I have grown so feeble?* The answers, Marlin says, are wrapped in the mystery of God. But one thing he knows for sure: God's timing is perfect even when we don't understand.

As I pull up a chair next to Marlin, my heart begins to stir up a deep truth. This dear elderly man practices a quiet acceptance of his circumstances. He sits in a wheelchair for hours each day; but in truth, he is walking humbly with his God.

Just as we are finishing our conversation, Marlin's face brightens. A double-amputee in a wheelchair has rolled up to his doorway. I watch a huge grin spread from ear to ear across Marlin's face. He calls the resident by name and gives him an encouraging thumbs-up. The man in the wheelchair beams, then rolls down the hall.

< 49 >

For me, it was a sacred moment lifted out of time. Though his earthly body fails him, Marlin has made peace with his predicament. I believe he understands that sometimes all you can do is quietly worship the One who is in control, then give away a smile to someone else who needs it. But it's enough. It's more than enough.

Numbers 6:26

May the LORD show you his favor
　　and give you his peace.

Prayer

O God of peace,
You know how I feel today. I am desperately searching for a reason to live. There seems so little I can contribute to this world. Yet your Spirit reminds me that I am never stronger than when I depend on you. Help me to be obedient until at last we meet, face to face. Amen.

< 50 >

Yvonne

Gentle spirit

* * *

Yvonne, a tiny sprite of a woman, is so petite you might think she'd blow away in a windstorm. But beneath her fragile exterior lies a steely faith. I know because I have witnessed it for decades.

With a halo of short curls framing her softly radiant face, Yvonne has a friendly, shy smile. An octogenarian, she still maintains a flawless sense of fashion, draping scarves and shawls around her shoulders in just the right way. She's certainly no diva though. You'll never find her calling attention to herself. She is quiet, reserved, and humble. It's hard to believe she once reared five children in a bustling household.

On many Sunday mornings, Yvonne greets members and visitors at the front door of the church with warm words or a tender embrace. On occasions when I have the opportunity to

< 51 >

stand next to her during a worship service, I always appreciate her worshipful heart. I can hear her voicing every word of the hymns we sing, the creed we recite, the congregational prayers we say.

Later as we sit down to talk, I am careful to speak into her "good" ear, knowing that a hearing loss has made conversation difficult for her at times. Now that her husband of six decades has passed away, she admits she gets lonely at times. They had been the perfect team for so long. Still, Yvonne knows that the older you become the more losses you likely will endure. So she continues to move forward, taking life a day at a time. Each step of the way, she quietly pours herself into the lives of others.

Yvonne is living out the end of life the same way she has lived the rest of her life—with a gracious spirit and a gift of hospitality. Somehow she manages to find the good in each person. As any member of her large extended family will tell you, she offers grace again and again. Hers is the gentle voice that encourages and affirms, no matter the circumstances. Hers is the spirit that makes others feel special.

< 52 >

With Yvonne, there is no fanfare. She is a petite woman with an enormous heart for God. What fills her heart is on her lips. Grace. Amazing grace.

1 Peter 3:4

You should clothe yourselves instead with the beauty that comes from within, the unfading beauty of a gentle and quiet spirit, which is so precious to God.

Prayer

Dear Lord and Father of us all,
Shine through me that I might be a gentle light in the world. Where there is chaos, let me be a holy calm. Where there is emptiness, let me pour out your love and grace. Amen.

< 53 >

Mary

Making a joyful noise

* * *

Not long ago, my eighty-seven-year-old friend Mary and I shared a piano bench at her assisted-living center. I opened a hymnal and began playing some of her favorite hymns. It didn't matter that the piano had not been tuned in years or that I could reach down and pick up the unattached pedals in my hand. We laughed out loud and went right on singing. Even though Mary is nearly blind, she sang with great confidence, taking the melody line while I sang harmony. We spent an hour having an old-fashioned hymn sing, just the two of us.

I first got to know Mary at the retirement community where she and my parents had been neighbors. Back then she always wore an oversized visor and counted her steps to compensate for her diminishing vision caused by macular degeneration. She had never learned

< 54 >

how to read music, but she could bang out gospel tunes on the piano for the ecumenical Sunday school class held at the center. But a series of health complications weakened Mary, and she moved to another facility to receive additional care. Now she spends most of her time sitting in a recliner, surrounded by family photos that she can no longer see.

On the afternoon of our sing-along, Mary hummed when lyrics suddenly escaped her and grinned all the while. For those of us who, like Mary, grew up in Sunday school and church, singing familiar hymns reconnects us to our faith and revives positive memories. By the time we got to the chorus of "Shall We Gather at the River," Mary was tapping her fingers and moving her feet while I did my best to keep up on the rickety piano.

On the drive home I thought about Mary and God's purpose for her in these late years. In some ways it seems there is little she can offer. She is frail. She can't see. She can't remember things like she once did. But somehow I knew that our hymn singing was more than recalling days gone by. We were glorifying the One who

< 55 >

ordained her long life. We were praising God in the here and now.

And so Mary sings despite the walker she needs to get around, despite her blindness. Despite dependence on caregivers for basic needs, Mary still sings her faith. That's when something wonderful happens. There is joy! The sweetest sound of all.

Psalm 32:11

So rejoice in the LORD and be glad, all you who
    obey him!
Shout for joy, all you whose hearts are pure!

Prayer

Loving Creator,
Sometimes it seems my body can barely sustain life. Then I remember that you know exactly how I feel. When weariness settles over me, I will make music. When my enthusiasm for living begins to fade, I will sing your praises. From the chair in my room I will worship you. Amen.

< 56 >

Nora Lee

Harvesting life

* * *

When I called Nora Lee to set up a time for us to visit, I had to leave a message on her answering machine. It turns out she'd been outside all afternoon, picking up pecans from a stand of twenty-two pecan trees on her property. Knowing Nora Lee's strong work ethic, I should not have been surprised to learn that she and her brother had gathered fifty-two pounds of pecans that day. Even at age eighty-four, Nora Lee is not one to waste time staring mindlessly at television reruns when there is life to be lived.

In the almost thirty years I have known Nora Lee, she has typically operated at one speed: full throttle. If she's not quilting or baking, she's probably exercising with a group of seniors or volunteering at church or in the community. But don't make the mistake of thinking Nora Lee is more a Martha than a Mary in the biblical

< 57 >

sense. Like Martha, she does a yeoman's work. But like Mary, she pauses to sit at the Teacher's feet and learn. She takes her Bible study, Sunday school lessons, and prayer life very seriously. Even so, you'll not hear her spout lofty theological language. She is plainspoken and smart, living out her unshakable faith honed by real-life experience.

On the day we meet for lunch Nora Lee reminds me that exactly four months have passed since her husband of sixty-three years passed away. After a brief melancholy moment, her face lights up as she reminisces about the three-week honeymoon she and her husband took in a borrowed car. A few minutes later she seems visibly more vulnerable, talking about the first night she spent alone following her husband's death. It's evident that she misses his sense of humor and his companionship. Before long she's proudly updating me on members of her close-knit family, including college professors, teachers, professional musicians, and a minister.

When I ask Nora Lee about her perspective on aging, she recounts a recent story that reveals her outlook on this stage of life. It seems a woman questioned her about going

< 58 >

to the movies not long after her husband died, implying that Nora Lee was not grieving appropriately. Nora Lee reminded the woman that it was her husband who died, not her, and that she was getting on with living. As soon as she completes her comment, she flashes me a quick smile that says in spite of loss, she chooses to live each day with purpose and resolve.

During the time we are sitting in the café, I watch Nora Lee discreetly acknowledge more than a dozen other patrons with a half-smile or a nod of the head. When we finish the last bite of dessert, the waitress announces that someone has already paid our bill. Seeing the surprise on my face, Nora Lee laughs and assures me that it happens all the time in her small town. I'm thinking that it probably happens more often to someone like her.

One thing is certain: Nora Lee's faith is not a casual thing. Though she glimpses life experiences in the rearview mirror, she does not dwell in the past. She has made the decision to fully live out the end of a life that has long been saturated in faith. Later, as I prepare to leave her home, Nora Lee asks me to wait a moment. She

< 59 >

goes inside and returns with a homemade cake. Chances are she has made it with the pecans she's picked herself.

It gets me thinking again about the pecans on the ground in Nora Lee's grove. If no one ever cares enough to pick up the pecans, they could never be used to create her luscious desserts. I smile to myself and think, *Isn't that just like Nora Lee? Still harvesting life's riches for others to enjoy.*

James 3:17-18

But the wisdom that comes from heaven is first of all pure; then peace-loving, considerate, submissive, full of mercy and good fruit, impartial and sincere. Peacemakers who sow in peace raise a harvest of righteousness. (NIV)

Prayer

Lord of harvest,
You are the source of all good things. You have given us the earth, the sun, and the rain. May my life bear witness to your goodness and bring forth a bountiful harvest. Amen.

< 60 >

Jim

A cowboy's calling

* * *

It's easy to picture Jim in a John Wayne movie. He has that rugged look you'd expect of a cowboy who still saddles up occasionally to work a herd of cattle. With a weathered, masculine face and seventy-one years under his western belt, he is the real deal.

For much of his youth Jim was involved in rodeos, even riding bulls while in high school. He served in Vietnam and later was a sheriff's deputy before becoming a game warden and then earning a degree in criminal justice. Now that Jim has retired, he spends time doing what he genuinely loves to do—repairing saddles and boots at his leather shop in a small town.

With this cowboy there is no swagger, at least not since he experienced a moment of spiritual clarity a few years ago. According to Jim, there had been a dryness in his soul like a tumbleweed

< 61 >

on a windswept prairie. In carrying out his law enforcement jobs, his heart had become hardened by years of dealing with the darker shades of life. Even though he had been involved in church since childhood, he gradually had drifted away from an intimate relationship with his Creator. It took a God intervention at a spiritual retreat to get the full attention of this aging cowboy.

Today Jim's boots are planted on solid ground. After fully submitting his life to God, he now has a renewed sense of purpose. He is a lay speaker for his church. He also participates in a weekly accountability group. Drawing from his rich experiences in the outdoors, he even writes and performs country gospel music and cowboy poetry in which the authenticity of his heart is clearly evident.

Not long ago Jim discovered an unexpected way to use his guitar and his heart for ministry. When visiting his elderly mother-in-law in a senior care center in another town, he realized how many other residents needed someone to come alongside and encourage them. As he formed relationships with the older adults, Jim began to bring his guitar, inviting residents to

< 62 >

sing along to favorite hymns. Sometimes he would even draw on his background as a lay speaker and offer a brief message.

On returning to his hometown, Jim approached his minister about initiating a senior care ministry at his church. Now six other church members assist him in regular visits to care centers and homebound members. They sit and talk, pray and share Communion with those who can no longer attend church services.

Most of the people Jim visits are frail and have difficulty articulating thoughts and feelings, but their faces brighten as soon as he strums songs of faith. For many residents, it is a rare message of hope: one older adult extending his calloused hand to another.

Colossians 2:2

My purpose is that they may be encouraged in heart and united in love, so that they may have the full riches of complete understanding, in order that they may know the mystery of God, namely, Christ. (NIV)

< 63 >

O God,

Remind me that even though I am growing older, I can still minister to others. Though I sometimes fumble for words, you can use me to encourage those with less strength and stamina. Show me how to use my gifts so that others will know you. Amen.

< 64 >

Gwen

No pity parties allowed

* * *

One morning each month Gwen grabs the keys to the church van and slides into the driver's seat. The seventy-nine-year-old woman welcomes a dozen or so other older adults as they climb on board for another outing she's planned for them. Gratefully she's been blessed with good vision and mental sharpness so that she is able to drive the group safely to visit interesting sights within a thirty-mile radius of their town. She doesn't do big-city driving, but she says there are plenty of places to see close to home.

Not long ago the group visited a restored one-room schoolhouse. Another time, they learned about alternative energy at a wind farm. Topmost in their minds is lunch at a café or diner somewhere along the way. Still, for Gwen and the others, the outings are about more than

< 65 >

sightseeing and eating out. They are about good-natured bantering, fellowship, and faith building.

As the leader of the pack, Gwen fully understands the needs of her older-adult peers. For years she has chaired the congregational care ministry at her church. In fact, if she's not baking casseroles to put in the freezer to have on hand when someone in the church family has a need, she's likely visiting the homebound or working in the church's mission store. Her two grown sons tell their own stories about their mother's passion for church life. They learned at an early age that if they found a cake sitting on the kitchen counter, they dare not cut into it because it probably was intended for someone in need or for a church event.

Not surprisingly, Gwen is a self-proclaimed doer, not a sitter. She's not about to become a couch potato, and she's not drawn to a rocking chair. Perhaps her need for activity has to do with surviving the deaths of two husbands. Her first husband died unexpectedly at a young age. The second succumbed to cancer after he and Gwen had been married for a number of years.

In this new season of life, Gwen clearly focuses on living. The way she sees it, faith

< 66 >

enables a person to adjust to each stage of life. Take it as it comes, she says. Embrace both the good and the bad, and keep moving forward.

No matter what, Gwen refuses to throw herself a pity party. She won't dwell on aches and pains of growing older. Instead, she sets her sights on family get-togethers or getaways to her lake house where younger neighbors have embraced her youthful attitude and vivacious spirit. She never fails to get back home for Sunday morning service that anchors her for another week's activity.

Looking back on her life, Gwen says it's easy to recognize God's hand in the circumstances of the past. Sometimes God has prodded her to visit someone in need. Sometimes she felt a nudge to pick up the phone and call a shut-in. Giving herself to others is what keeps her going. Look for Gwen at the gas station, filling up the church van. It's time for another outing.

Luke 6:38

"Give, and you will receive. Your gift will return to you in full—pressed down, shaken together to make room for more, running over, and

< 67 >

poured into your lap. The amount you give will determine the amount you get back."

Holy God,
My life is not my own. I belong to you. Let me embrace this day, humbly serving others with my time and gifts. Guide my thoughts and words, that in all I do, you will be glorified. Amen.

< 68 >

Lester

Full of years, full of grace

* * *

Each morning Lester wakes up and reaches for the framed photograph of his wife. He gives it a kiss and remembers their long life together. They had been married sixty-eight years when she succumbed to Parkinson's disease. For more than a decade, he had been her daily caregiver. Now, at one hundred years old, he looks at his own longevity as an unexpected gift, despite the loss that inevitably comes with it.

Early one Sunday morning Lester and I met in the narthex of the large church where he worships. Even before we were introduced, Lester's ministers had told me how he inspires others to live more faithfully. He joins in placing informational materials in the sanctuary's three thousand seats each week and actively

< 69 >

participates in a Sunday school class. But I was most fascinated to learn that Lester also regularly volunteers alongside other church members at a homeless shelter in the inner city.

I asked Lester what advice he would give to younger older adults. He didn't even catch his breath before cautioning others not to shut themselves off from the world. It became quickly apparent too that he takes his own counsel. In addition to his volunteer work at church, Lester is committed to daily exercise. He walks about two hours each day. Not surprisingly the former grain elevator manager prefers to get his exercise outside where he can enjoy nature. When the weather doesn't cooperate, he walks inside a local mall. The important thing, Lester says, is to keep moving.

Though Lester knows he has been blessed with good health, he believes that training his mind has had a lot to do with his longevity. He refuses to dwell on fear or uncertainty. Every day he reads at least one chapter from the Bible, and he prays for family members by name. He also makes a point to surround himself with music that lifts his spirits as he counts his many blessings.

< 70 >

As Lester and I share time together, I realize that he has discovered the secret of growing old gracefully is really no secret at all. It is recorded in scripture for anyone to see. Stay connected to the community of faith. Serve others. And set your mind on things above.

Colossians 3:2

Set your minds on things above, not on earthly things. (NIV)

Prayer

O Lord,
My life is full of years. I have outlived so many friends and family, but I am blessed with a treasure trove of memories. Though my steps are slow, let me keep moving for you, serving others for you, until at last I stand in your presence. Amen.

< 71 >

Betty R.
A second wind

* * *

Sitting on Betty's red-and-white-checkered sofa, I look over at her perfectly coifed hair and try to imagine her as a youthful goalie for her school's field hockey team. With two brothers and natural athletic skill, she was quite the tomboy in her youth. Not only did she excel at field hockey, she played basketball and softball and was a roller-skating champ. I am trying to visualize my sweet eighty-four-year-old neighbor playing stickball in the street when she begins the story about how she met her future husband while sitting on a pool table.

In her words, she had gotten all gussied up to go to the USO where a friend was singing for the soldiers. Her high-heeled shoes began to pinch her feet, so she decided to give her aching feet a rest. With no available chairs, she jumped up onto the pool table. About that time a friend passed by

< 72 >

and introduced her to a handsome military man who would become her husband two years later.

For many years now Betty has been my neighbor. Since her husband of over fifty years passed away, Betty has found comfort in the companionship of her miniature dachshund. In spite of loss and life transitions, you will not hear Betty complain. She even lives with the complications of scoliosis the way she does everything else—with acceptance and humor.

On most Thursday mornings Betty is the first to arrive at the bazaar workshop at our church. She puts on the coffee and sees that tables are set up before the dedicated women arrive to work on handcrafted items to be sold in early November. These are not glue-gun crafts; they are handsome artisan objects. Betty quickly points out that the funds made from the bazaar are distributed to various missions, both local and global. Just last year, the bazaar raised $24,000.

When I playfully mention that some of the older men in the church refer to the women of the bazaar workshop as "bizarre," she raises her brow and howls in laughter. The twist on words is a familiar joke repeated by men who

< 73 >

contribute their woodworking skills to the effort.

Betty works on bazaar projects year-round, specializing in embroidered and other hand-stitched items. This work has become more than a personal outlet. It is her mission—using her hands to create objects that ultimately will help others. To Betty's way of thinking, life is short, so why not use it to benefit people and have some fun and fellowship while you are at it?

When she feels sluggish or unmotivated, Betty often senses an inner voice telling her to get up and do something in service to others. Her spirit is renewed. It seems to be her second wind.

Proverbs 11:25

The generous will prosper;
> those who refresh others will themselves be
>   refreshed.

Prayer

O Spirit God,
In this twilight of my life, set my heart on fire.
Send a second wind to renew my spirit that I
might live to serve your people. Amen.

< 74 >

Jimmie Tom

On the wings
of prayer

* * *

A surprising eighty-five years old, Jimmie Tom welcomes bank customers into his office with a boyish grin and eyes that twinkle behind his wire-rimmed glasses. In the best old-fashioned sense he is a true gentleman, gracious and engaging. Since he has no children of his own, Jimmie Tom is everyone's granddad or favorite uncle, I learn.

To look at him across the desk, you'd never know that he has survived multiple heart surgeries. He seems youthful and trim, a condition perhaps attributed to a regular exercise regime at a rehabilitation center where he has made many late-in-life friends. Though he works at the bank only a few mornings a week, Jimmie Tom believes staying active is key to aging well. Older adults in the community often come to

< 75 >

him for financial advice because he has earned their trust and respect over the years. Some need assistance reviewing their bank statements. Others turn to him for expertise in sorting out their financial futures.

Actually Jimmie Tom had never intended to pursue a career in banking. After a stint in the military, he returned to college before heading to the big city. Eventually the bank in his hometown asked him to step into a leadership position. The rest, as they say, is history. But Jimmie Tom has no regrets. In fact, he calls moving back to his hometown answered prayer.

For Jimmie Tom, prayer is not just something you mutter before a meal or when a crisis looms. He has made prayer a lifetime habit of candid conversations with God throughout the day. There's no fancy language, he says—just plain talk about events of the day or decisions to be made.

Aside from his own aging, Jimmie Tom understands firsthand the challenges of growing old. Some years ago, he served as the primary caregiver for both his elderly parents. His mother had Alzheimer's; his father battled chronic health issues. Toward the end of their lives,

< 76 >

Jimmie Tom moved into their home so he could better care for their daily needs. In a bittersweet way, he still finds comfort in knowing that they died only six days apart.

Folks in Jimmie Tom's hometown are quick to say he is a sincere and humble witness of his faith. Though he likely would be embarrassed by their accolades, those who know him best describe his life as exemplary. Even as he continues to age, Jimmie Tom reminds others not to wish away their long lives, telling them to look at life as a gift. Be grateful for each day and remember to thank the One who gives.

Before I leave Jimmie Tom's office, he gives one last piece of advice for those who drone on about the misery of aging: don't do it. Don't complain. Find ways to keep connected to life; give back to the community. Most of all, pray.

Psalm 17:6

I am praying to you because I know you will
    answer, O God.
  Bend down and listen as I pray.

< 77 >

Prayer

O God,

I reflect on all that you have done in my life, and I am thankful. I will pour out my heart to you because you listen to me. I can talk to you anytime, anywhere. Lying in bed. Sitting in a wheelchair. Resting in an easy chair. Hear me now, O Lord. Amen.

< 78 >

Daisy

What's in a name?

* * *

Daisy's name seems a perfect fit. Like the flower with petals radiating from a center disk, she is a ray of sunshine, even at eighty years old. It's little wonder that people at her senior residence center are drawn to her wide grin and friendly ways.

In many ways Daisy's gregarious personality seems contradictory to the insecurity she's experienced since childhood. Brought up in a military family, she attended fourteen schools before graduating and had little opportunity to nourish long-term friendships. By the time she was thirty-two, she had two young daughters and was recovering from a heartbreaking divorce. Not long after, she borrowed money to finish college and earned a teaching degree. Then at age thirty-eight she married again. It was a marriage that lasted almost four decades before her husband died.

< 79 >

As Daisy tells it, a life-changing moment recast her life direction. She had always attended church, but it wasn't until she and her husband participated in a laity retreat that she suddenly realized she'd known *about* God without really knowing God personally. When she finally allowed her emotions to connect with her intellect, Daisy had an epiphany, a turning point in her life that affected every relationship in a positive way.

Indeed Daisy's journey toward spiritual maturity continues to make a difference in the lives of her fellow residents at the retirement community who are drawn to her warmth and humor. As much as she loves to talk, she's learned to practice the art of listening to her peers. She engages residents in conversation about their frustrations and fears, their joys and celebrations. She reads to those whose vision is faltering. She shares books or jokes with those who need a lift. It is her ministry: lavishing attention and acts of compassion on others.

On the day when I visit, we sit in the dining room of her retirement center. As lunchtime draws to a close, I count eleven people who

< 80 >

have stopped by the table to talk to Daisy. These are not folks who just spoke a pleasantry as they strolled by. They stopped at our table and patiently waited for a lull in our conversation so they could talk to Daisy. They chatted easily about everything from diabetic shoes to the names of famous poets. No matter the topic, it was apparent that each resident was drawn to Daisy because she makes every one feel special.

When I asked Daisy about her thoughts on aging, she didn't even pause before answering: find something to laugh about each day. Make a point of being around people, but also allow time alone to reflect on God's goodness for all you've experienced in your long life.

Not long ago I read something interesting about daisies in the gardening section of the newspaper. Certain varieties of daisies bounce back soon after they've been mowed down. That sounded a lot like Daisy! No matter her circumstances, she keeps popping back up, reaching for the sun, and putting a smile on the face of others.

< 81 >

1 Thessalonians 5:11

So encourage each other and build each other up, just as you are already doing.

Prayer

Encouraging God,
Let me hear the voices of your people today. Give me words that will lift them up out of the pit of loneliness or fear. Let me give them special care that they might find comfort in knowing they are loved. Amen.

< 82 >

Edith

Being content where you are

* * *

The first time I saw Edith, she was wearing a fuzzy robe and standing on the porch of the humble frame house she shared with her husband. It was a cold December night, and I was part of a church group singing Christmas carols door-to-door. Until then, I had only known Edith's husband, a faithful member of my own congregation. I had not met Edith, who was active in another local church.

A few years after that first meeting, Edith's husband became quite ill. From time to time, I would stop by to visit. The more time I spent with her, the more evidence I saw of her mature faith. She lovingly cared for her life partner. I was drawn to her character and gracious spirit. Over time we developed a deep friendship that would continue long after her husband of sixty years passed away.

< 83 >

For many years Edith was a hairstylist on the town square, although she says *beautician* was the term used back in her day. The way she tells it, life was fairly simple then. She and her husband worked hard, loved their daughter, and lived contentedly. To this day, she has rarely traveled far from the place where she was reared.

Now ninety-four years old, Edith faces a recurrence of cancer. As I pull up a chair next to her comfortable recliner, I am inspired by the way she continues to find contentment amid the uncertainties of life. She talks glowingly about the flowering vines outside her door. She recalls a recent trip to the lake with her son-in-law. Then she says something I will forever remember. In a clear voice, she exclaims that everything she has ever wanted in life can be found right where she is.

Somehow I know it is true. Edith's life is centered on things that have lasting value— faith, family, and friends.

Not long ago I began thinking of all the changes in the world that have occurred during Edith's lifetime. When she was young, there were only dirt roads and horse-drawn wagons in her farming community. Now there are

< 84 >

luxury cars and six-lane highways. Innumerable electronic gadgets and medical advancements have evolved over these years. I was reminded that while others get sidetracked by a pursuit of things bigger and better, Edith keeps her eyes clearly focused on things that are eternal. She lives a life free of hypocrisy and selfish greed. There is much to be learned from her about finding contentment in one's own circumstances.

As I prepare to find the scripture verse to accompany Edith's story, I open my Bible and turn to the book of Timothy. There nestled in the pages is a needlepoint bookmark Edith made for me a while back. Two words stitched in blue: *be grateful.* Edith is living proof that contentment comes with a grateful heart. She lives a simple life worthy of her calling. There in a humble frame home lives one of the richest people I have ever known.

1 Timothy 6:6

Godliness with contentment is great gain. (NIV)

< 85 >

Prayer

God of all good gifts,
My years have been filled with wonderful
memories of friends and family. All that I ever
really need is you, O God. Help me to find
contentment in my present circumstances
knowing you are with me always. Amen.

< 86 >

Bob

Back from the brink

* * *

Several years ago Bob was told he had only fifteen minutes to live. Overwhelmed with pain, he had just walked into an emergency room where a nurse wisely recognized his symptoms. Within a few brief moments, a surgeon informed him he had an abdominal aortic aneurysm. Immediately he was whisked away for six hours of surgery. Bob survived and somehow knew that life would never be the same.

Now at age seventy-eight Bob knows that time is precious. He makes a conscious effort to count his blessings every day. On most mornings he puts on his belt, thanking God that he can still reach behind his back to pull it through the loops. He is grateful to be alive. Almost dying can do that to a man.

The aneurysm was not Bob's first encounter with death. At the age of five he was suddenly

< 87 >

orphaned when his parents were killed in an accident. An only child, he was later adopted and reared by an older couple. In spite of a rough start, Bob chose to focus his life story on happier times: getting married, serving in the air force, completing his college degree, and having three children. When the youngest child was in high school, a crisis struck again. His wife died of cancer.

Eventually Bob found love and married again. Over the years, he and his wife followed a career path that took them to several different states. Not long after he retired, he stumbled upon a unique ministry that drew on his business experience with computers. It started when Bob went to visit a friend in a retirement community. When he arrived, his older friend was talking with a repairman who'd come to fix his computer. After the repairman left, Bob and his friend reviewed the repair bill. Bob realized there probably had been a less expensive solution to his friend's computer problem. Fearing that other older adults might be targets of unscrupulous practices, Bob began offering his time and expertise to help less knowledgeable seniors solve their computer woes.

< 88 >

Bob emphasizes that most of the older adults he assists primarily use their computers for e-mail correspondence and for viewing family photos online. Nothing gives him more satisfaction than restoring files for an older adult who thought every photo and e-mail message had been lost forever. Their smiles and tears of joy are payment enough.

Indeed, when Bob gets up each morning, he's already fixed his mind on his projects for the day. He has an ongoing list of those who need his expertise. Most people discover Bob's unique ministry by word of mouth from other residents at senior care centers or from church. In his spare time, Bob heads up his church's senior fellowship group.

Bob knows what it is to stand on the brink of death. He knows what it is to be given another opportunity to live. He doesn't understand the mystery of it all, but it is an opportunity he will not squander.

< 89 >

Ecclesiastes 3:1-2

For everything there is a season,
> a time for every activity under heaven.

A time to be born and a time to die.
> A time to plant and a time to harvest.

Prayer

God of all time,
There's so much about life and death we do not understand on this side of heaven. You have numbered my days and given them purpose. Let me embrace this season of life that I might glorify you and give myself to others. Amen.

< 90 >

Barbara

Bubbling over

* * *

Barbara can best be described as effervescent. With oversized glasses and a mile-wide grin, she bubbles like fine champagne. On most Sunday mornings you can hear her laughter reverberating through the hallways at church.

Though Barbara is wonderfully vivacious, her life has not been spared from heartache. She has survived cancer and has outlived two husbands in her eighty-seven years. She was unable to have children, but she has countless friends and family members who, attracted to her quick wit and warm personality, adore her. Just being in her presence for a short while makes you thankful for the gift of a new day.

On the day we meet to talk, Barbara is waiting on a plumber to fix a leaky faucet. Regarding the matter as just another little annoyance in life, she takes it all in stride. When I ask her the secret

< 91 >

to living a long, happy life, her eyes twinkle. Her two-phrase answer says it best: keep moving! Keep living.

This animated octogenarian is serious about keeping active. She is so serious, in fact, that she goes square dancing at least twice a month at a local community center. After her second husband died of a heart attack, Barbara knew she needed to be around people. When she saw a promotion for a square dance club in the newspaper, she jumped at the chance to join a family of fun-loving seniors who link arms and sashay around the room. Square dancing has other benefits too, she points out. Learning and remembering the calls keeps her mind alert, and the two-and-a-half-hour sessions provide great exercise.

On Wednesday mornings Barbara trades in her square dancer's petticoats for business attire. She heads for her city's police department where she regularly volunteers. Having completed a required course and background check, she can assist with tasks like copying and folding communication bulletins and shredding documents. The best part of her volunteer position, though, is interacting with staff members—everyone from the police

< 92 >

chief to the newest rookie cop. She derives great satisfaction in knowing she supports her city in a small way.

When I get up to leave Barbara's home, she opens her arms and engulfs me in a huge bear hug. I can't help but think that the world could use a lot more Barbaras. Her attitude goes beyond optimism. Barbara looks at each moment as an opportunity to extend God's heart to others. No wonder a sweet scent of joy trails behind her.

Proverbs 15:30

A cheerful look brings joy to the heart;
   good news makes for good health.

Prayer

O God,
I confess there are times when the grumps get me down. There are moments when I complain to anyone who will listen. Breathe your spirit into this old body and help me find joy. Give me purpose for another day. Amen.

< 93 >

Scotty and Louise

Blest be the tie that binds

* * *

On the second Saturday of each month Scotty and Louise gather with family members for breakfast at a local café. What started as an occasional event has become a tradition the older couple anticipates with great joy. On any appointed Saturday, the number of attendees fluctuates, but every adult child, grandchild, and spouse ranks the monthly get-together as a top priority. There's always room too for any of the great-grandchildren. Except for one granddaughter's family currently overseas, family members all live within a sixty-mile radius.

To ninety-four-year-old Scotty and ninety-year-old Louise, the breakfast tradition is not about omelets and pancakes. It's a special way

< 94 >

to keep the family connected face-to-face in a busy world. To other family members, it's about valuing time with their aging loved ones.

Scotty and Louise look at their family and marvel at their blessings. Both are cheerful and grateful for a long life, noting that family and faith keep them going. They delight in the latest stories about activities of the grandkids and great-grandkids. For them, the greatest benefit of growing old is more opportunities to be with family. As they say, what we leave behind when we die is our influence on others' lives.

After seventy-three years of marriage, it's no wonder there's an easy banter between Scotty and Louise. Versions of the story about their first meeting may differ, but whether Scotty was delivering newspapers or playing football in a vacant lot, once he saw Louise, he was smitten. They married and brought up four children.

After Scotty retired as an executive of a large metropolitan car dealership, he and Louise crisscrossed the country in their RV. Nowadays they stick closer to home since both contend with major health issues. Even so, they both have interests that keep their minds active.

< 95 >

Scotty researches the family genealogy on the computer. Louise cross-stitches a quilt for every new great-grandchild. Both keep up with current events. Neither one dwells on the uncertainty of tomorrow. As Louise explains, if we are worrying about tomorrow, we can't live for today. Both have embraced this late season of life and intend to live it fully. They are showing others how to grow old gracefully. Love is the glue that holds a family together, and faith is the tie that binds.

Ecclesiastes 4:12

A person standing alone can be attacked and defeated, but two can stand back-to-back and conquer. Three are even better, for a triple-braided cord is not easily broken.

Prayer

God of all generations,
Thank you for the love of family. With you in our lives, our bond is strengthened so that it is not easily broken. Even on difficult days, let me celebrate the tie that binds generations. Amen.

< 96 >

Nelle

I'll fly away

* * *

Nelle has already planned the music for her memorial service. She has made it clear to family members that she wants her grandson to bang out a toe-tapping rendition of "I'll Fly Away" on the piano while everyone sings along. It seems fitting for this spirited eighty-seven-year-old woman who still mows her own yard and balances her checkbook to the penny.

I have known Nelle for many years since we have a close mutual friend. Over time our paths have intersected at many celebrations and events. A few years ago I watched Nelle interact with my friend's aging parents and thought her to be the quintessential friend—fiercely loyal, compassionate, and giving. When my friend's elderly folks were in fragile health, Nelle visited them daily, checking on their safety and well-being. Though she was ten years their junior,

< 97 >

they had been longtime friends. She cooked their favorite soups, played cards with them, and took them on outings. Since they have passed away, Nelle continues to model authentic friendship, nurturing several younger adult neighbors in similar ways.

On the day we meet to talk, I am reminded of just how stunning Nelle is. It's easy to visualize her as the high school cheerleader and homecoming queen she once was. It is more difficult to imagine her as the highly skilled fisherman her family knew her to be.

When I ask Nelle about marriage, a huge smile breaks across her face. She tells about marrying her high school sweetheart just days after he returned from a stint in the United States Navy. On their wedding day, the temperature soared to 103 degrees. The heat in the un–air-conditioned church caused all the candles to melt. Somehow, though, I doubt that even an oven-baked wedding bothered the unflappable Nelle too much. Now widowed after forty-four years of marriage, she delights in spending time with her daughter, two grandsons, and a heap of great-grandchildren.

< 98 >

When our conversation shifts to the tough realities of aging, Nelle's eyes draw me like a magnet. Her tone grows serious. To her way of thinking, there's no excuse for older adults to sit around and feel sorry for themselves. Longevity is a gift, she says, in spite of the hard times. Taking her own advice, Nelle has become an avid sports fan, tracking her favorite teams on television to feed her interest. She also reads, works crossword puzzles, and tends to her many flowers and potted plants.

One thing that has changed as Nelle has aged is her prayer life. In the past, she says, she mostly prayed for God to do things for her or for one of her loved ones. Nowadays her prayers flow from a grateful heart. Looking back, she sees evidence of God's hand in her life in countless situations. She offers thanks for her blessings. In return she receives clarity and a positive outlook on life.

Just before I leave, Nelle casually mentions her schedule for the rest of the week. There's lunch with a neighbor, soup to make for a friend, a Sunday school lesson to study, and a great-grandchild's school event. I smile as I think to

< 99 >

myself, *At least it's winter, so there's no need for her to mow.*

Galatians 6:9-10

So let's not get tired of doing what is good. At just the right time we will reap a harvest of blessing if we don't give up. Therefore, whenever we have the opportunity, we should do good to everyone—especially to those in the family of faith.

Prayer

O God,
When I feel like giving up, refocus my mind
on all that is good in life. Use me to encourage
others along this journey. Help me keep my
eyes on you and not on the uncertainties of life.
Amen.

< 100 >

Roger

The spiritual
journey continues

* * *

Early on a Monday morning I slip into a back pew in the empty sanctuary of Roger's church. It seems an appropriate place to talk with the eighty-three-year-old man who admits that growing old has brought him closer to God and to the church. His fascinating life story would remind anyone that a spiritual journey does not end with old age.

In many ways Roger's childhood set the course for the rest of his life. He recalls a tender deathbed conversation with his ailing father when he was only six years old. Still an impressionable child, Roger remembers making a pledge to live an honorable life.

Not long after his father died, Roger and his mother moved to a different city to be near an uncle. Soon Roger began selling newspapers to

< 101 >

earn extra money. When Roger begins to recall his high school years, he suddenly sits up a little straighter. He takes special pride in his school's involvement with paper drives and saving bond sales to benefit the country's effort during World War II. He reports that the students' projects were so successful they were recognized in national publications. It was in this season of life that a fire of patriotism was first stoked in Roger's heart.

Eager to serve his country during this time of global conflict, Roger convinced his mother to sign papers that would allow him to join the United States Navy at the age of seventeen. Before long he was assigned to a submarine chaser in the Pacific. He remembers with great clarity his commanding officer making an announcement forever etched in Roger's mind: "Never forget those who have sacrificed their lives on behalf of this great country." Roger has not.

At the conclusion of his military service, Roger completed college, married, and set out on a career path that would take him to a pinnacle of technological advancement. Perhaps it was a matter of fortunate timing when Roger played a vital role in establishing the earliest computer

< 102 >

programs for a large oil company. He became a pioneer in computer technology, participating in mind-boggling changes over the last half century. Along the way, Roger and his wife divorced, but today he remains close to his two sons and five grandchildren, who live not far away.

As our discussion turns to issues of faith, Roger admits that as a younger man he was often disturbed by the hypocrisy he saw among Christians, especially those who leave their professed faith at the church door on Sunday morning and forget about it until the following Sunday. Soon, though, I notice a softening in Roger's eyes. The tug of faith is strong as he continues his life journey.

Roger is thankful for the opportunity to think more deeply about God in his later years and to be more sensitive to the needs of others. Admittedly it makes him sad to think that younger generations don't have the same sense of patriotism shown by his generation. He worries too about greed and selfishness permeating the nation.

As I drive out of the church parking lot, I wave one last time to Roger. He is walking toward the church's garden to assist with the

< 103 >

Food Chain ministry that provides vegetables for people in need. I think to myself, *There goes an honorable man who is taking another step on his spiritual journey.*

Proverbs 8:17-18

I love all who love me.
    Those who search will surely find me.
I have riches and honor,
    as well as enduring wealth and justice.

Prayer

God of life,
As I grow older, I think about the world my grandchildren will inherit. Help me to pass on eternal values to them. Direct every step of my spiritual journey and bring me closer to you. Amen.

< 104 >

Janice

Prescription
for aging well

* * *

On many Sunday evenings Janice walks into the church toting a plastic carryall along with her Bible and study manual. Inside the carryall is one of her melt-in-your-mouth cakes. Before long, class participants are standing in line, waiting to get a slice of Janice's homemade delicacy. Everyone knows she is a great cook who loves to bake for others.

At age seventy-four, Janice is also a wise woman who knows that interacting with friends and family does a lot to lift her spirits and keep her mind active. She finds great friendship among a group of fellow retired school employees who meet monthly. She also turns to her church family for spiritual and emotional support. Each year Janice participates in several Bible studies in addition to attending a senior adult Sunday school class and a monthly fellowship group.

< 105 >

For many years Janice has lived alone. She understands both the freedom and the danger of independent living. On some days, it is tempting to stay inside, especially if the weather is not cooperative. To counteract that temptation, Janice makes a point of getting outside the house for a while every day. She may go to the YMCA or to the grocery store. She may take a walk or work in the yard. She knows the danger of drawing the blinds and isolating herself from other people.

I sink into Janice's sofa one afternoon, and we begin to chat about her interesting Norwegian heritage. When I inquire about the rural community where she was born, she brings out a photo album with pictures of her family's homestead, now designated a historical landmark. Time flies as she shares heartwarming stories of her parents and grandparents, her sons and grandchildren, of travels to the Holy Land and to Scandinavia.

It doesn't seem surprising that Janice worked as a registered nurse. Her compassionate caregiver's heart soon becomes evident to anyone around her. In her younger days Janice worked in hospitals before taking a position as a nurse in a local school district for more than

< 106 >

two decades before retiring. For years I have heard that even the most rebellious high school students were won over by Janice's pleasant but firm ways.

As the late afternoon sunlight slips away, I look at Janice's sweet face and realize that she is never one to draw attention to herself. Instead, she draws people in and makes them glad to be around her. It seems she has found a great prescription for aging well.

Colossians 3:12

Since God chose you to be the holy people he loves, you must clothe yourselves with tenderhearted mercy, kindness, humility, gentleness, and patience.

Prayer

Compassionate Father,
As I grow older, remind me that the best medicine is being with others. Nurture me in becoming a person whom others enjoy being around. Show me each day what it is to age well. Amen.

< 107 >

Virginia

Living until the end

* * *

I've often thought that when I grow old, I want to be like Virginia. At eighty-six, she's still got a keen intellect and a sense of humor that rivals any twenty-year-old college student. Instead of reviewing her long life and asking how much longer she must endure, Virginia tries to figure out how she can pack more living into each new day.

Widowed in her early fifties, Virginia has lived alone in her own home for more than three decades. But she is not one to sit in an easy chair and simmer in her aloneness. In fact, she claims that the best antiaging medicine is to keep living full speed ahead.

During the last few years Virginia has researched and written the history of her local church, documenting stories and photographs for a hardbound book. She specializes in

< 108 >

genealogy and speaks to groups about the history of the community where she grew up and still lives. When she's not writing or speaking, she's likely volunteering at her church. She also sings with the older adult choir and plays folk instruments in a band that performs at senior centers and churches in the area.

Often you'll find Virginia sitting at her computer. Though she took a few computer classes at the local community college, she is mostly a self-taught computer whiz kid. Through trial and error she's even found a way to add voice-overs and background music to DVDs she made from old 8mm movies.

The point is, Virginia doesn't hold life at arm's length. She pulls it close and squeezes every moment of the day. She knows her body is destined to grow old, but she works to keep her mind alert and curious as an expression of her faith. I guess that's why I hope to be like Virginia when I grow old. Living fully until the very end.

1 Corinthians 15:58

So, my dear brothers and sisters, be strong and immovable. Always work enthusiastically for the

< 109 >

Lord, for you know that nothing you do for the Lord is ever useless.

O God,
Forgive me for the times I refuse to get out of my easy chair and engage the world. There is still so much to learn. Let me draw from your boundless wellspring of creativity. Prompt me to discover something new today. Keep my mind curious and alert, according to your will. Overcome my fear with courage, and turn my boredom into opportunity. Let me live a vibrant life until my last breath. Amen.

< 110 >

About the Author

Missy Buchanan, a former creativity educator, lives in Rockwall, Texas, with her husband, Barry. She is the author of the best-sellers *Living with Purpose in a Worn-Out Body: Spiritual Encouragement for Older Adults* and *Talking with God in Old Age: Meditations and Psalms.*

Missy writes a monthly column, "Aging Well," for *The United Methodist Reporter.* She has written articles for many publications, including *Presbyterians Today, Response, Mature Years,* and *Good Morning America's Weekly Inspiration.*

Missy speaks regularly to older adult groups, churches, and women's groups, and has appeared on *Good Morning America* with cohost Robin Roberts and her mother, Lucimarian Roberts. Missy has a special place in her heart for older adults after serving as a daily caregiver for her parents in their last years.

Visit her Web site: www.missybuchanan.com.

< 111 >